JOAN OF ARC

JOAN OF ARC
MAURICE BOUTET DE MONVEL

INTRODUCTION BY GERALD GOTTLIEB

A STUDIO BOOK

THE PIERPONT MORGAN LIBRARY *AND* THE VIKING PRESS · NEW YORK

INTRODUCTION

It was a cruel and brutal time; and it was a sad time for France. The year was 1429. The Hundred Years' War was almost over. The endless battles and skirmishes in which the French fought the English or the Burgundians had devastated the lovely countryside of France. The land was ravaged by soldiers who marched back and forth across it on their murderous errands, burning fields and looting villages as they went. Roads were overgrown; brigands roamed the forests; travel between towns was very dangerous.

The kingdom of France was ruled by the Dauphin Charles, whose father, King Charles VI, had suffered bouts of madness before dying. There were those who said that the Dauphin's real father had been not King Charles VI but the king's brother, and therefore the Dauphin was not the legitimate heir to the throne. His mother the queen would neither deny nor confirm the rumor. The Dauphin consequently lived in great self-doubt and guilt, and he could not muster up the courage to have himself crowned.

And the war was going very badly for the French. All the country north of the Loire was controlled by the enemy—the English under John, Duke of Bedford, and their allies the Dukes of Burgundy. Paris itself was in the hands of the English. Orléans, the city that was the key to the Loire Valley and the gateway to the entire south, was under heavy siege. French armies had suffered a long string of defeats and were feeble and demoralized. Orléans seemed doomed. And when this last citadel fell, nothing would prevent the enemy from sweeping south beyond the Loire and overrunning all the rest of the French kingdom.

At this moment, the darkest in the history of France, a miracle took place. It began in Lorraine on the eastern frontier, in a small piece of territory controlled by Robert de Baudricourt, a captain loyal to the French ruler. A seventeen-year-old peasant girl—uneducated, but in the grip of a profound faith in God, and very insistent—had come to Baudricourt talking of visions and voices. She claimed that the figures of saints appeared before her, lit by a beautiful light, and that she heard their voices. They spoke to her often, and with great urgency, and they told her that she had been chosen to save France from its enemies. They bade her drive away the army besieging Orléans and take the Dauphin to Rheims, where he would be crowned King of France.

Robert de Baudricourt was, to say the least, skeptical. For a long time now, a prophecy had traveled about the countryside and through the villages; it said that one day a young girl would come to rescue France. And many a young woman had deluded herself that she could fulfill the prophecy. They all seemed mad, but this young girl, who was named Jeanne d'Arc—Joan of Arc —was different somehow. People took her seriously. Even some of the veteran soldiers under Baudricourt believed in her. To Baudricourt she said: "I am come before you from my Lord . . . my Lord wishes that the Dauphin be made king . . . and it is I who will take him to be crowned."

"Who is your Lord?" Baudricourt asked.

"The King of Heaven," Joan answered serenely.

And when he finally agreed to send her to the Dauphin, she said: "I was born to do this."

How do we know these things? Much of our information comes from eyewitnesses who testified at the two great trials of Joan of Arc, and whose words are preserved in the detailed, copious trial records. The first of these two proceedings was the Trial of Condemnation, in 1431, which led to Joan's execution for heresy; and the second was the Trial of Rehabilitation, which began in 1450. By then Joan had been dead for nineteen years, but many people, high and low, who had known her personally were still alive. The story that emerges from the trial records and from other contemporary chronicles and documents is not a long one. Joan the Maid, as she came to be known, was taken by Baudricourt's men to the French royal court. There she promptly recognized the Dauphin Charles, though he was disguised as one of his own courtiers. They spoke together in private, and she won his confidence immediately. What she said to him is not known, but it is likely she told the fearful, self-doubting monarch that she knew for certain he was the legitimate ruler of France, and that she had been sent by God to have him crowned. Joan was then tested by an ecclesiastical court, and she convinced the high churchmen that she was not a sorceress, that Saints Michael, Catherine, and Margaret *did* appear to her, and that she did indeed hear their voices and converse with them. And then she went on to her great triumphs, leading and inspiring French troops to victories, first at Orléans, where the enemy besiegers were driven off and the city liberated, and then at one fortress after another along the Loire Valley, culminating in a great rout of the enemy at Patay. Obeying her voices, she then achieved her dream of bringing the Dauphin to Rheims, where she saw him crowned King Charles VII of France. With her curious mixture of blind bravery and naïve gentleness (she loved the banner she carried in battle "forty times more than her sword"), Joan gave the French a new confidence and pride. She told them: "In God's name the soldiers will fight, and God will give the victory." She fanned a flame of patriotism in France that would burn forever. She became truly beloved of the multitude.

The nobles of the court, however, were less enthusiastic about the Maid; and Charles VII, his kingdom more secure now, had little further need of Joan. But the Maid still heard her voices, and she was still possessed by a burning urge to drive the enemy from the soil of France. She led troops in an attempt to take Paris from the English. The attempt failed. By now Joan had acquired a taste for fine clothing, and for masculine attire. She would dress in the elegant clothes of a nobleman of the court; she would go into battle wearing a splendid, flowing robe over her armor. Fighting in a skirmish at Compiègne, she suddenly found herself surrounded. A Burgundian soldier seized her robe and dragged her from her horse. She was taken prisoner. No one came forward to rescue or ransom her. The French king and his court watched and did nothing as the Burgundians sold her to the English. (The price was high—ten thousand livres.) The English announced that Joan the Maid would go on trial as a witch and a heretic.

The trial could have but one possible outcome. The English had bought her to burn her, and in the end nothing less would satisfy them. Joan of Arc died at the stake in the city of Rouen in May, 1431. Ten thousand people crowded into the square to watch. Some of the onlookers said later that when the executioners lit the fire a white dove flew up from the center of it. Others claimed that, outlined in the flames, they had seen the letters J E S U S. And the old chronicles tell of still other wondrous things, for as the flames rose above the pyre in Rouen, so rose up the legend of Joan the Maid, the savior of France. Upon that legend were nurtured French courage and hope, and a new feeling of unity. That, in the end, was the achievement of Joan of Arc.

Such are the bare bones of the story. Joan of Arc was a visionary—devout, energetic, stubborn, ignorant but intelligent, gifted with military genius, and aflame with her mission. She became France's national heroine. In 1896 a fellow countryman of the Maid, an artist named Louis-Maurice Boutet de Monvel, set out to celebrate her achievements in a book for children. By then, of course, Joan had been revered in France for nearly five centuries. There had been countless illustrated versions of her story, for children of every age. But Boutet de Monvel now managed to create a new masterpiece. His *Jeanne d'Arc* would be more admired and loved, and would influence more artists and illustrators, than any other children's book of its era.

Boutet de Monvel was born in 1850 in Orléans, a city that had been obsessed with Joan of Arc ever since the Maid delivered it from siege in 1429. As a boy in Orléans he saw the name of the young heroine everywhere—on streets and squares, on public statues, on boxes of candy. The boy became an art student, and by 1874, at the age of twenty-four, he was an academic painter, exhibiting at the Paris annual Salon. Early in his career he turned to the illustration of magazines and books for children, and here he enjoyed success both financial and artistic. (At the same time he pursued another career, with even happier financial results, becoming international society's painter of choice for portraits of children.) Among the children's books he illustrated in the 1880s was *La Civilité puérile et honnête,* a work on etiquette for the young in the manner of the French courtesy books, which had a history going back to the Middle Ages (though Boutet de Monvel's treatment was somewhat tongue-in-cheek). He also illustrated a selection of La Fontaine's *Fables.* In both works he demonstrated an ability to reconsider and reinvigorate a time-worn theme, to take a traditional subject and make something new of it.

This ability came into play again in 1896, when he took as a subject the figure that had been omnipresent in his Orléans childhood—Joan of Arc. Inspiration, he later wrote, came to him in Paris, as he stood in the Place des Pyramides before the gilded statue of the Maid, stiff and erect on her charger, brandishing her sword toward the Tuileries. The theme, even the inspiration, were hardly new. But Boutet de Monvel, with his special talent for quickening the traditional, produced a series of pictures that would be his *chef-d'oeuvre,* his own monument to the Maid.

For this new children's book he not only painted the pictures but also wrote the text. And a comment is perhaps necessary here about that text. Boutet de Monvel, it must be remembered, was a painter, not a writer. Even less was he a scholar; and consequently some of the facts in the book have been called into question. But it must also be remembered that Boutet de Monvel's *Jeanne d'Arc* was a work of its time. It should be judged as such. Consider the book's title page, upon which the Maid, in mediaeval armor, leads eager French riflemen dressed in the uniforms of 1896. Presumably she is leading them to a victory, one that perhaps will help the nation forget the defeat suffered by French arms in the Franco-Prussian War of 1870–71. The battles listed on the standard the riflemen bear are those of Napoleon's pre-Waterloo triumphs. Boutet de Monvel is calling for, or dreaming of, a resurgence of the military glories won by not only Joan the Maid but also the Emperor Napoleon. Nor is this title-page propaganda absent from the pages that follow, even though they are set in the Middle Ages. Boutet de Monvel's pictures may depict the fifteenth century, but his writing is infused with the nationalistic fervor of the 1890s. One can hardly expect to find in it the balance, the measured reason of an ideal historian.

So much for Boutet de Monvel the writer. Boutet de Monvel the artist is quite another matter. The text of *Jeanne d'Arc* may be flawed, but pictorially the book is a work of genius. It was recognized as such from the very first. "Unique," one critic called it. Indeed it was; but its images were rooted in the past. Although the flat, shadowless coloring of the pictures was reminiscent of Japanese prints (which had been much in vogue in France, witness Gauguin), or of children's paintings, many of the images had a more distant source. It was certainly a more logical source, for it was contemporaneous with the Maid herself. We know that Boutet de Monvel read mediaeval chronicles—Froissart, no doubt, and Monstrelet—from which he surely took the events, the dramatic confrontations, of his *Jeanne d'Arc*. But did he not perhaps also pore over the illuminations in mediaeval manuscripts? The massed groupings of men and horses, the stylized backgrounds, and above all the opulent detail of robe and wall hanging, are all to

be seen in illuminated manuscripts from early fifteenth-century France, the time and place of the Maid's life. They can be seen, for example, on the vellum leaves of the *Très Riches Heures du Duc de Berry,* illuminated by the Limbourg brothers, and in work that the Boucicaut Master produced for Charles VI, the father of Joan's feckless and ungrateful Dauphin.

However one may speculate about the pictorial sources of Boutet de Monvel's greatest creation, its influence was pervasive on the children's books that followed. That is why its pictures seem so familiarly modern to us today, nearly a century after the artist produced them to transport and inspire children and to do homage to the peerless heroine of his own childhood.

Boutet de Monvel's *Jeanne d'Arc* was originally published in 1896, in Paris. A copy of that first edition is among the rare early children's books in the collections of The Pierpont Morgan Library in New York. The present edition, prepared from the Morgan copy, is the first edition since the nineteenth century which faithfully reproduces Boutet de Monvel's extraordinary colors and compositions. It thus enables a new generation of children and adults to experience this important classic of book illustration in all the freshness and subtlety of its original colors and all the drama of its brilliant, moving scenes.

The French text written by Boutet de Monvel was first translated into English in 1897, by A. I. du Pont Coleman. The English text of the present edition is an adaptation of that translation. It has been modified for modern readers, but an effort has been made to retain the flavor of the nineteenth-century original.

Gerald Gottlieb
Curator of Early Children's Books
The Pierpont Morgan Library
New York City

11

Joan was born on January 16th, 1412, in Domrémy, a little village in Lorraine which was
under the rule of the King of France. Her father's
name was Jacques d'Arc, her mother's Isabellette
Romée; they were honest people, simple laboring
folk who lived by their toil.

Joan was brought up with her brothers and
sisters in a little house that is still to be seen in
Domrémy, so close to the church that its garden
touches the graveyard.

The child grew up there under the eye of
God.

She was a sweet, simple, upright girl. Everyone loved her, for all knew that she was kind-
hearted and was the best girl in the village. A hard
worker, she aided her family in their labors. During the day she led the animals to pasture or
joined her father in doing heavy work; in the
evening she sat spinning at her mother's side and
helped her with the housework.

She loved God, and she prayed to Him often.

One summer day, when she was thirteen years old, she heard a voice at midday in her father's garden. A dazzling light burst forth, and the Archangel Michael appeared. He told her to be good and to go to church often. Then he spoke of the pitiful condition of the Kingdom of France, and he told her that she would go to the help of the Dauphin and bring him to be crowned at Rheims. "Sire, I am only a poor girl," she said. "I could not ride a horse or command soldiers." "God will help thee," answered the Archangel. And the child, overcome, was left weeping.

From this day on, Joan's piety became even more intense. The girl loved to sit alone and meditate. She heard heavenly voices speaking to her, telling her of her mission. These, she said, were the voices of her Saints. Often the voices were accompanied by visions. Saint Catherine and Saint Margaret appeared to her.

"I saw them with my own eyes," she said later to her judges, "and when they left me I cried. I wanted them to take me with them."

The girl grew, her mind exalted by her visions. Deep within her heart, she kept the secret of these heavenly conversations. No one suspected what was happening inside her—not even the priest who heard her confessions.

At the beginning of the year 1428, Joan was sixteen. The voices became more insistent. The peril was great, they said, and she must go to help the King and save the Kingdom.

Her Saints commanded her to seek out the Sire de Baudricourt, Lord of Vaucouleurs, and to ask him for an escort to conduct her to the Dauphin.

Not daring to tell her parents about her project, Joan went to Burey, where her uncle Laxart lived. She begged him to take her to Vaucouleurs. Her fervent pleas overcame the fears of the timid peasant, and he promised to go with her.

Baudricourt's reception of her was brutal. Joan told him that God had sent her to bring word to the Dauphin to stand firm, for God would give him help before the middle of Lent. She added that it was the will of God that the Dauphin should become King, that he should be crowned in spite of his enemies, and that she herself would lead him to his coronation. "The girl is crazy," said Baudricourt. "Box her ears and take her back to her father."

Joan returned to Domrémy. Then, urged again by her voices, she came once more to Vaucouleurs and saw the Sire de Baudricourt again, but with no better welcome.

This time, however, she remained at Vaucouleurs. Soon nothing was talked of there but the young girl who went about saying openly that she would save the Kingdom, that someone must take her to the Dauphin, that God willed it. "I will go," she said, "if I have to wear my legs out doing it."

The simple-hearted people, moved by her faith, believed in her. A squire, Jean de Metz, was impressed by the confidence the people showed in Joan and he offered to take her to Chinon, to the court of Charles VII. The poor people somehow scraped together enough money to clothe and arm the little peasant girl. They bought her a horse, and on the appointed day she set out with a small escort. "Go, and take the consequences!" Baudricourt threw after her. "God keep you!" cried the poor people; and the women wept as they saw her go.

B.M.

Chinon was far away and the journey there was perilous. The enemy, both English and Burgundian, occupied the countryside. The little troop had to cross bridges held by the enemy. They had to travel by night and hide during the day. Frightened, Joan's companions spoke of returning to Vaucouleurs.

"Fear nothing," said she. "God is leading me, and my brothers from Paradise tell me what I ought to do."

So, on the twelfth day, Joan arrived at Chinon with her companions. From the hamlet of Sainte-Catherine she had addressed a letter to the King, announcing her coming.

The court of Charles VII was in disagreement about how to receive Joan. La Trémoille, the King's current favorite, wanted nothing to disturb the influence he had gained over his indolent master. For two days the council argued about whether the King should receive the inspired girl.

Then, suddenly, bad news came. Orléans, besieged by the enemy, was in danger of falling. The King's council, desperate, resolved to hear this girl who claimed to be a messenger from God. Perhaps she could help save Orléans. That evening, by the light of fifty torches, Joan was brought into the great hall of the castle, crowded with all the nobles of the Court. She had never seen the King.

Charles VII, so as not to attract her attention, wore a costume less splendid than that of his courtiers. At the first glance Joan singled him out. She knelt down before him. "God give you a happy life, gentle King!" she said. "I am not the King," he answered; "yonder is the King." And he pointed out one of his nobles.

"You are he, highborn prince, and no other," Joan said. "The King of Heaven sends you word by me that you shall be anointed and crowned." And she told him that God had sent her to aid him. Joan asked him for some soldiers and promised to raise the siege of Orléans and to bring him to Rheims.

The King hesitated. The girl might be a sorceress. He sent her to Poitiers, to have her examined by learned men and ecclesiastics.

For three weeks they tormented her with insidious questions. "There is more in God's book than in your books," she said. "I may not know my ABCs, but I come on behalf of the King of Heaven." When they objected that God did not need the help of soldiers to save France, she sprang to her feet and declared: "The soldiers will fight, and God will give the victory." And then, as at Vaucouleurs, the ordinary people declared their support of her. They felt that she was holy and inspired. The learned and powerful were forced to yield to the enthusiasm of the multitude.

The troops gathered at Blois. Joan arrived there with some of the French leaders. On her banner were embroidered the image of Christ and the names Jesus, Mary. She advised her soldiers to confess their sins before going into battle.

On Thursday, April 28th, with Joan at its head, her banner flying, the little army moved off, singing the hymn "Come, Holy Ghost." She wished to march straight to Orléans, but the leaders thought it more prudent to cross the Loire and approach the city from the south, through country held by the French.

The troops stopped just across the river from Chécy, two leagues from Orléans. They now had to cross the Loire, but they did not have enough boats. Joan crossed to the other bank of the river with part of her escort and the provision train. The rest of the troops were forced to go back to Blois, and from there try to reach Orléans by another route.

Count Dunois, who commanded the defenders at Orléans, came to meet Joan. She said to him: "I bring you the best of help, that of the King of Heaven. It comes not from me, but from God Himself. Hearing the prayers of Saint Louis and of Charlemagne, He has had pity on the town of Orléans."

At eight in the evening, Joan entered Orléans. The people crowded forward to meet her. She passed by torchlight through the city, in the midst of a throng so dense that she could hardly make her way. Men, women, and children wished to get near her or at least touch her horse, showing "as great joy as if they had seen God descend among them." It was as though the siege were lifted, so fortified were they by the God-given valor of the simple maid. Joan spoke softly to the people, promising to deliver them.

She asked to be taken to a church, wishing before all things to give thanks to God.

An old man spoke to her of the English: "My child, they are strong and well-entrenched, and it will be a hard matter to get rid of them." She answered: "Nothing is impossible to the power of God."

Her confidence inspired everyone around her. The people of Orléans, who the day before had been so timid and discouraged, were now so excited by her presence that they wanted to fling themselves on the enemy. But, fearing defeat, Dunois decided to wait for reinforcements before beginning an attack. In the meantime, Joan exhorted the English to give up the siege and go back to their own country. They answered her with insults.

Some time passed, but no news was received from Blois. Dunois, uneasy, went to Blois to hasten the arrival of reinforcements. He was just in time. The Archbishop of Rheims, Regnault de Chartres, the King's Chancellor, reversing the earlier decision, was about to send the troops back to their garrisons. Dunois obtained permission to lead them to Orléans.

On the morning of Wednesday, May 14th, surrounded by all the clergy of the city and followed by a great part of the population, Joan left Orléans and made her way through the English lines to meet Dunois' little army. They returned to the city, under the protection of priests and Joan, without the English venturing to attack them.

Later that same day, Joan, trying to rest, arose with a start. "Oh, my God!" she cried, "the blood of our men is flowing. Why did no one wake me? Quick, my armor, my horse!" Aided by the women of the house, she quickly donned her armor, leaped into the saddle, and galloped off, holding her standard aloft. Her horse's hooves struck sparks from the cobblestones as she rode straight for the fighting.

26

Without alerting Joan, the French had attacked the English bastion of Saint-Loup. The attack failed; the French were retreating in disorder. Joan rushed up, rallied them, and led them once more to the very foot of the bastion. The English, under their commander Talbot, fought back desperately for three hours, but despite their resistance the French overcame them and captured the bastion.

The victorious Joan returned to Orléans. But, in the joy of her success, as she crossed the field of battle she felt her tender heart melt with pity at the sight of the dead and the wounded that she encountered along the way, and she wept as she thought of those who had died without confession. The sight of French blood flowing always made her hair stand on end, she said.

Now the question was how to follow up this successful attack against the English.

The French leaders, reluctant to let themselves be commanded by a peasant girl, or to share with her the glory of success, met in secret to discuss the plan to be adopted.

Joan appeared before the council. The Chancellor of the Duke of Orléans tried to conceal the council's plotting. Joan became indignant at his subterfuges and cried, "Tell me what you have concluded and settled! I am well able to keep a greater secret than that!" She went on: "You have been at your council, and I have been at mine; and, believe me, God's counsel will be accomplished and will endure, while yours shall perish. Rise tomorrow very early, for I shall have much to do, more than I ever had before."

The next day, May 6th, she captured the bastion of the Augustinians. Then, very early on the morning of the 7th, the attack on the Tourelles bastion began. Joan was in the moat, raising a ladder against the parapet, when an arrow from a crossbow pierced her between her neck and shoulder. She pulled the iron shaft out of the wound. When someone offered to help her with a magic charm, she refused, saying that she would rather die than do anything contrary to the will of God. She made her confession, and she prayed a long time while her troops rested. Then, giving the order to begin the assault again, she threw herself into the thickest of the fight.

The bastion was captured, and all its defenders perished.

On Sunday, the English were positioned in order of battle on the north bank of the river. Joan forbade any attack on them. When Mass had been celebrated, she said to those about her: "Look and see if the English have their faces toward us, or their backs." And when she was told that they were retreating in the direction of Meung, she said: "In the name of God, if they are going, let them go. It is not the pleasure of our Lord God that you should fight them today. You shall have them another time."

So Orléans, besieged for eight months, was delivered in four days.

The news of the deliverance of Orléans spread far and wide, attesting in the sight of all to the divinity of Joan's mission.

Shunning the gratitude of the people of Orléans, the holy maid returned hastily to Chinon. She desired to profit from the enthusiasm stirred up around her by going at once to Rheims, taking with her the King in order that he might be crowned. The King received her with great honors, but he refused to follow her. He accepted the devotion of the heroic girl, but he had no intention of letting her efforts, however noble, disturb the shameful indolence of his royal existence. It was decided that Joan should go to attack the positions still held by the English on the banks of the Loire.

On June 11th, the French occupied the suburbs of Jargeau. The next day, at dawn, Joan gave the signal for battle. The Duke of Alençon wished to delay the assault. "On, gentle Duke," she cried, "to the attack! Doubt not, this is the moment chosen by God. Work, and He will work with you!" And she mounted the scaling-ladder. She was thrown down by a stone which struck her on the head, but she rose, crying to her men: "Up, up, friends! God has doomed the English! They are ours already! Take heart!" The ramparts were scaled, and the English were taken prisoner or killed. On June 15th, the French captured the bridge of Meung. On the 16th they laid siege to the town of Beaugency; and on the 17th the town surrendered.

On June 18th, near Patay, Joan faced the English army under Talbot and Falstaff.

"In God's name, we must fight them," she said. "Even were they to hang from the clouds they would not escape from us, for God sends us to chastise them. Our noble King shall have this day his greatest victory yet!" And she tried to join the vanguard, but her men restrained her. La Hire was ordered to attack the English in a holding action, to give the French reserves time to come up. But his onslaught was so impetuous that everything gave way before him. When Joan rode up with her men-at-arms, the English were retiring in disorder. Their retreat became a rout, and Talbot was captured.

"You did not think, this morning," said the Duke of Alençon to him, "that this would happen." "It is the fortune of war," Talbot answered.

Four thousand English were killed and two hundred were captured. No mercy was shown except to those who could pay a ransom; the rest were put to death without pity.

One of them was struck down so brutally that Joan leaped from her horse to help him. She raised the poor man's head, brought a priest to him, and comforted him in his dying. Her heart was as full of pity for the English wounded as for her own supporters.

Joan constantly exposed herself to blows, and she was often wounded, but she never wished to use her sword; her standard was her only weapon.

The French took the city of Troyes. The English and Burgundian soldiers there were granted the right to leave the city with all their possessions, which consisted principally of French prisoners. In drawing up the terms of surrender, nothing had been said on behalf of these unfortunates. But as the English left the city, leading their captives with ropes round their necks, Joan threw herself across their path. "In God's name," she cried, "you shall not take them away." She insisted that the prisoners be delivered up to her, and that the King pay their ransom.

On July 16th, the King entered the town of Rheims at the head of his troops. The next day the coronation ceremony took place in the Cathedral, before a great throng of nobles and commoners. Joan placed herself behind the King, with her standard in her hand. When Charles VII had received the holy unction and

the crown from the Archbishop, Regnault de Chartres, Joan threw herself at the King's feet, clasping his knees and weeping hot tears. "O gentle Sire," she said, "now the pleasure of God has been accomplished. He willed that I should bring you to your city of Rheims to receive the holy anointing which shows that you are truly King, and that to you must belong the Kingdom of France." All those who saw her at that moment believed more than ever that it was a thing come from God. "Oh the good, devout people!" cried the holy maid, as she saw the enthusiasm of the people crowded round the king. "If I must die, I should be most happy to be buried here."

Nothing was so touching as the devotion of the common people to Joan. They vied with one another to kiss her hands or her clothes, or just to touch her. They brought little children to her that she might bless them; brought rosaries and holy images for her to sanctify by the touch of her hand. And the humble girl graciously rejected these signs of adoration, gently teasing the poor people for their blind belief in her power. But she asked at what time the children of the poor went to communion, so that she might go with them. She had pity for all who suffered, but she had a special tenderness for children and for the lowly. She felt like a sister to them, knowing that she came from among them. Later on, when she was reproached for permitting this adoration of the multitude, she would answer simply: "Many people were glad to see me, and they kissed my hands when I could not prevent it; but the poor people came freely to me because I never did anything to harm them."

After the coronation at Rheims, Joan wished to make a sudden descent on Paris and recapture the capital of the Kingdom. The King's indecision gave the English time to prepare their defense. The assault was repulsed; Joan was wounded in the thigh by an arrow. They had to drag her away from the foot of the ramparts to make her abandon the conflict. The next day the King was unwilling to renew the attack, though Joan promised him success. He had been on the march long enough; he was impatient to resume his indolent life at court.

This retreat, forced upon her by the weakness of Charles VII and the jealousy of his courtiers, was a terrible blow to Joan's prestige. Henceforth, she ceased to be invincible in the eyes of all. The holy maid seems to have understood this, for before quitting Paris she left as a votive offering on the altar of Saint Denis her hitherto victorious arms. She prayed long. Perhaps she had a presentiment that her glorious mission was ended, and that sad trials were in store for her.

Nevertheless she submitted and, heartsick, she followed the King to Gien. The army was disbanded, the courtiers feeling that there had been enough fighting. Moreover, their jealousy made it imperative for them to put a stop to Joan's successes.

But Joan could not resign herself to the inaction that they wished to impose upon her. She finally realized that she must henceforth expect no aid from Charles VII. At the end of March, 1430, without taking leave of the King, she went to Lagny to rejoin the French forces that were skirmishing with the English.

Now during Easter week, after she had heard Mass and received communion in the church of Saint-Jacques at Compiègne, she withdrew, leaned against a pillar of the church, and wept. She said to some of the townsfolk and children who surrounded her: "My children and dear friends, I tell you that they have sold and betrayed me, and that I shall soon be delivered up to death. I beg you to pray for me, for nevermore shall I have power to help the King and the Kingdom of France."

On May 23rd, at Crépy, she learned that the town of Compiègne was closely surrounded by the English and the Burgundians. She went thither with four hundred men, and entered the town at daybreak on the 24th. Then, taking with her a part of the garrison, she attacked the Burgundians. But the English then attacked, and the French fell back. "Think of nothing but striking them!" cried Joan. "Their defeat lies in your hands." But she was borne away by her retreating men. When they reached the ramparts of Compiègne again, they found the drawbridge raised and the portcullis closed against them. At bay in the moat, Joan still fought on. An entire

enemy troop fell upon her. "Surrender!" they cried. "I have sworn and given my faith to Another," answered the brave girl, "and I will keep my vow to Him." But her resistance was in vain. Pulled by her flowing garments, she was dragged from her horse and captured. From the ramparts of the town the Sire de Flavy, Governor of Compiègne, saw her taken, but he did nothing to help her.

45

Joan was brought to Margny, amid the joyful shouts of her foes. The English and Burgundian leaders, even the Duke of Burgundy himself, pressed forward to see the sorceress. They found themselves in the presence of a girl of eighteen. She was the prisoner of Jean de Luxembourg, a penniless gentleman, who wished only to make a good profit from his prize. The King of France made no offer to ransom her.

Joan was imprisoned in the Castle of Beaurevoir. Knowing that the English wished to buy her from the Sire de Luxembourg, and also that the siege of Compiègne would result in the capitulation of the town, she slid down one night from the top of the keep with the help of leather strips. They broke; she fell to the foot of the rampart and lay there as though dead. She recovered from her fall, however; an end more cruel was reserved for her. Late in November she was delivered to the English for the sum of ten thousand livres.

Shut up in the dungeon of the castle at Rouen, she was guarded day and night by soldiers, whose insults and even brutality she was forced to bear, her chains not allowing her to defend herself. Meanwhile a tribunal, controlled by the English and presided over by Cauchon, Bishop of Beauvais, was preparing her trial. Against the insidious questions of her judges the saintly maiden, without support or counsel, had no defense but her virtue and the purity of her intentions. "I am sent by God," she said. "I have nothing more to do here. Send me back to God, from whom I came."

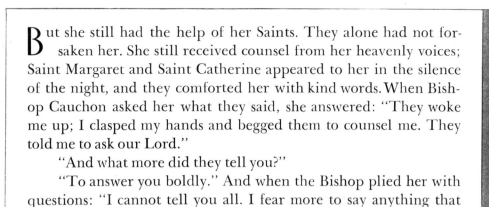

But she still had the help of her Saints. They alone had not forsaken her. She still received counsel from her heavenly voices; Saint Margaret and Saint Catherine appeared to her in the silence of the night, and they comforted her with kind words. When Bishop Cauchon asked her what they said, she answered: "They woke me up; I clasped my hands and begged them to counsel me. They told me to ask our Lord."

"And what more did they tell you?"

"To answer you boldly." And when the Bishop plied her with questions: "I cannot tell you all. I fear more to say anything that might displease them than I fear you."

One day the Earls of Stafford and Warwick came to see her with Jean de Luxembourg. When the latter jestingly said that he came to ransom her if she would promise never again to bear arms against the English, she answered: "In God's name, you are mocking me, for I know that you have neither the wish nor the power to save me. I know the English will put me to death, expecting after I am gone to win the Kingdom of France; but if they were a hundred thousand more, they should not have the Kingdom."

The Earl of Stafford, enraged, threw himself upon her, and would have killed her had not the others intervened.

Joan, treated as a heretic, was deprived of the consolations of religion. The sacraments were denied her. Returning from an interrogation, and passing with her escort before the closed door of a chapel, she asked the monk at her side whether the body of Christ lay within. She implored him to let her kneel for a moment and pray. He consented; but Cauchon, hearing of it, threatened the monk with the direst punishment if such a thing occurred again.

The trial went too slowly to please the English. "Judges, you are not earning your pay!" they cried to the members of the tribunal. "I came to the King of France," said Joan, "on the part of God and the Church Triumphant in Heaven. To that Church I submit myself, my works, and all that I have done or shall do. You say that you are my judges; take good heed what you do, for truly I am sent by God, and you put yourselves in great peril." The saintly heroine was condemned, as a heretic, to be burned alive in the old marketplace of Rouen. "Bishop, I die because of you!" she said to Cauchon.

On May 30th, Joan went to confession and received communion. Then she was conducted to the place of execution. When she reached the foot of the scaffold, she knelt down and invoked God, the Virgin, and the Saints. Then, turning to the Bishop, the judges, and her enemies, she begged them devoutly to have Masses said for her soul. She mounted the pyre, asked for a cross, and died in the flames, the name of Jesus on her lips. All were weeping, even the executioners and the judges. "We are lost! We have burned a saint," cried the English, as they fled from the place.

Library of Congress Cataloging in Publication Data
Boutet de Monvel, Louis Maurice, 1850-1913.
Joan of Arc.
(A Studio book)
Translation of Jeanne d'Arc.
SUMMARY: A biography of the peasant girl
who led the French army to victory against the
English and paved the way for the coronation of King
Charles VII. This is a facsimile of the original 1896 French
edition.
1. Jeanne d'Arc, Saint, 1412-1431—Juvenile literature.
2. Christian saints—France—Biography—Juvenile
literature. [1. Joan of Arc, Saint, 1412-1431.
2. Saints] I. Title.
DC103.5.B6813 1980   944′026′0924 [B]   80-5169
ISBN 0-670-40735-6

Printed in Japan by Dai Nippon Printing Company, Tokyo
Set in Baskerville

The plates in this book were n **2522 7301 19** a's photographs of the
illustrations in the c   anne d'Arc.